BRAIN BUSTERS

BRAIN BUSTERS

Rosalind Woodman

Christian Focus Publications

(c) 1992 Christian Focus Publications

ISBN 1 871676 41X

Published by
Christian Focus Publications Ltd
Geanies House, Fearn, Ross-shire,
IV20 1TW, Scotland, Great Britain.

Cover design
by
Seoris N. McGillivray.

Printed and bound in Great Britain by
Cox & Wyman Ltd, Reading, Berks

The version of the Bible to be used in solving
the puzzle is the New International Version

CONTENTS

INTRODUCTION

Pit your wits, rack your brains and crack the codes as you work your way through this challenging puzzle and quiz compilation.

Whether you are young or old, have an extensive or a limited Bible knowledge, there is something for you.

Each section contains brain teasers on a variety of subjects from birds to books of the Bible. You can complete these on an individual basis, or test your knowledge in team contests.

Whether you are part of a church group, Christian Union or simply 'going it alone' we hope that you will enjoy hours of entertainment with **Brain Busters**.

SECTION ONE

QUIZZES

1. GENERAL KNOWLEDGE (1)

1. Which wood was used to build Noah's ark?
2. Which tree withered at Jesus' command?
3. Which name given to Jesus Christ means 'the end'?
4. What was the name of the memorial of deliverance in battle set up by Samuel between Mizpah and Shen?
5. Which church in the book of Revelation is noted for its lukewarmness and self-righteous spirit?
6. Whose son became lame in both feet when his nurse dropped him as a child?
7. Who was instructed by God to marry an adulteress?
8. In which two books of the Bible is the Tree of Life mentioned?
9. Who was 969 years old when he died?
10. Which was the first of the nine plagues mentioned in Exodus?

11. Why were the descendents of Anak to be feared?

12. Which two cities were destroyed by God with those of Admah and Zeboiim?

13. How old was Joseph when he was sold into slavery?

14. Why was Zecharias, the father of John the Baptist struck dumb?

15. Who took Judas Iscariot's place among the twelve disciples?

16. Name three instances when Jesus raised people from the dead.

17. In which book of the Bible do we find an account of St Paul's conversion in his own words?

18. On which occasion is Paul first mentioned in the Bible?

19. Who said that if all the things Jesus did were recorded, the world itself would not contain all the books that would be written?

20. How many times did Jesus cleanse the temple?

2. GENERAL KNOWLEDGE (2)

1. Who had a coat woven without a seam?
2. In the book of Ruth, what name did Naomi give to herself and why?
3. In Jeremiah's prophecy, who was going to come up against Jerusalem and take it?
4. How many psalms are there?
5. What did Elijah leave behind when he was taken up into heaven?
6. Whom did God instruct to set aside for his work together with Paul?
7. In Proverbs, which jewel is the wife of noble character worth far more than?
8. In the Old Testament, what was Belteshazzar's other name?
9. What is the fifth commandment?
10. At the time of the Passover, what were the Israelites instructed to paint on the top and both sides of the door frame, and with what?

12

11. Who sent for cedar, pine and algum logs from Lebanon and why?

12. What was the difference between John's baptism and Jesus's?

13. Where did seven of the disciples go fishing after the first Easter?

14. What did Jesus instruct ten lepers to do in order to be healed?

15. What are the three epistles to Timothy and Titus called and why?

16. In which village was Jesus' head annointed with expensive perfume?

17. Who were Eliphaz, Bildad and Zophar?

18. When the Israelites were in the wilderness, how often were they instructed to gather manna?

19. Name two occasions when we are told that Jesus wept.

20. Who was murdered because a king desired his vineyard.

3. INITIALS (1)

1. Name two people in the Bible whose names begin with F.
2. What P is the name of the place where Jacob wrestled with God?
3. What B is the pool where an invalid was healed by Jesus?
4. What B, which means 'confounded', was built on a plain in the land of Shinar?
5. What A was worshipped in Ephesus?
6. Which L was a tax collector?
7. M is the mountain on which Solomon's temple was built.
8. Which Z was priest at the time when Solomon was king?
9. Which G was Paul's teacher?
10. Which O was the son of Ruth and Boaz?

11. Which G is the place where Jesus delivered the demon-possessed man?

12. What P mentioned in the book of Esther is the feast celebrated by the Jews to commemorate deliverance?

13. Which N was the commander of the army of the King of Syria who was afflicted with leprosy?

14. Which D was the god of the Philistines?

15. Which I is the name of a baby born on a day of great calamity?

16. What S is the name of a resting place of the Ark of the Covenant?

17. Which C was Simon's other name?

18. What P is the island where John received a revelation?

19. Which M was Esther's cousin?

20. Which U was Abraham's birth place?

4. INITIALS (2)

1. What T involved living in booths for seven days, and commemorated forty years of wandering in the wilderness?
2. Which Z is the name of the town to which Lot escaped before the destruction of Sodom and Gomorrah?
3. What M is the name of the place where Moses struck a rock and water gushed out?
4. What A is the name of the cave where David sought refuge when pursued by Saul?
5. What J is the Bible city known as the city of palms?
6. What S is the king's name which means peaceable?
7. What J is a king who came to the throne at the age of eight?
8. What T was the name of David's beautiful daughter?

9. What M is the country where Elimelech and Naomi settled during a famine in Bethlehem?

10. What L is the tribe of Israel who had no allotment or inheritance?

11. What N is the mountain on which Moses died?

12. What D is the name of a tribe of Israel?

13. What B was a god worshipped by the Israelites during times of disobedience?

14. What P is the person to whom Paul wrote a letter about a runaway slave?

15. What M was a king of Salem and a priest of God?

16. What P was a servant of the church in Cenchrea?

17. What X is the king who made Esther his queen?

18. What H was one of Noah's sons?

19. What U is the land where Job lived?

20. What J was Barnabas's other name?

5. MEN OF THE BIBLE (1)

1. Which prophet was seen hundreds of years after he left the earth?
2. Who was the cousin of Barnabas?
3. Apart from Joshua, name another person who left Egypt and saw the Promised Land?
4. Who was threshing corn when he received a visit from an angel?
5. Who commanded the sun to stand still?
6. Which king took his own life?
7. Who was the first person to die, in the Bible?
8. Who wrote the last book of the Bible?
9. Who was the first Christian martyr?
10. Which prophet restored a boy to life after he had died of sunstroke?
11. Which king ruled at the time when Daniel was thrown to the lions?

12. Jethro the Priest of Midian was whose father in law?

13. Who was the Emperor of Rome at the time when Jesus was born?

14. Who owned a staff which sprouted, budded, blossomed and produced almonds?

15. Who had a gallows made and then hanged on them himself?

16. Which prophet shares the same name as David's second son?

17. Of whom was it said that it would have been better if he had never been born?

18. Who was high priest at the time of Jesus's crucifixion?

19. Which Old Testament character's name meant hairy?

20. Who was the brother of Martha and Mary?

6. MEN OF THE BIBLE (2)

1.   Who read the writings of a prophet while riding in a chariot?
2.   Who was commanded by an angel to fasten his belt and put on his sandals?
3.   Who came to Jesus by night?
4.   Which king pretended to be insane in an enemy country?
5.   In the Old Testament, who killed 1,000 people with a jaw bone?
6.   To whom did Paul refer as his own son in the faith?
7.   Which runaway slave was sent back to his master?
8.   Which prophet was a shepherd of Tekoah?
9.   Whose name meant 'laughter' and why?
10. Who hid 100 prophets to prevent them from being killed?

11. Who entertained three angels beneath a tree?

12. Who pleased God so much that he didn't see death?

13. Whose name meant 'Son of Encouragement'?

14. Which proud king was punished by God till his hairs were grown like eagle's feathers and his nails like bird's claws?

15. Who did God send to minister to Paul following the encounter on the Damascus road?

16. Which apostle was martyred by the sword by order of Herod?

17. According to the New Testament story, how was Eutychus killed?

18. Who was told in a vision to send men to Joppa for Simon Peter?

19. Who was compelled to carry Jesus' cross to the place of crucifixion?

20. Name the Macedonian who travelled to Rome with Paul.

7. PROFESSIONS

1. Name three tentmakers in the Bible.

2. Name two tax collectors.

3. Who was a shepherd and dresser of sycamore trees?

4. A lawyer.

5. Name the archer who was the ancestor of a great nation.

6. A cunning hunter.

7. A nurse who was buried under an oak tree.

8. A king who was also an extensive farmer.

9. A circuit judge over Israel.

10. A mighty hunter.

11. An inventor of string and wind instruments.

12. A tanner who lived in Joppa.

13. The name of a Roman Centurion who, on the instruction of an angel, sent for Peter.

14. The name and profession of a woman who met Paul by the river at Philippi.

15. The name of a silversmith mentioned in the book of Acts.

16. An evangelist from Caesarea who had four unmarried daughters who prophesied.

17. A prostitute who hid some spies.

18. Which of the apostles were fishermen?

19. A gardener.

20. A cup bearer.

8. ANIMALS AND BIRDS

1. Which animal spoke to his master?
2. Which animal killed a disobedient prophet?
3. Name one of two birds used for sacrifices.
4. Job owned three thousand of these animals. What were they?
5. Samson burned his enemies' cornfields by tying what animals together by their tails and putting torches in their knots?
6. To which bird did David compare Saul and Jonathan?
7. Which king traded in apes and peacocks?
8. When the prophet Elijah called down a curse on mocking youths, which animals were used to fulfil the curse?
9. On which occasion did God employ birds as messengers of mercy?
10. Which prophet asks if a leopard can change its spots?

11. Who said that God made his feet like the feet of a deer?

12. According to Isaiah's prophecy, which animal will lie down with the goat?

13. What was the second plague on the Egyptians?

14. Which two animals may be eaten for the Passover festival?

15. Which animal did Elijah sacrifice before the priests of Baal on Mount Carmel?

16. During the march around the walls of Jericho trumpets were blown. From which animal were they made?

17. What did John the Baptist eat?

18. Where does it say that the ostrich lays her eggs in the sand to be hatched in the heat?

19. Who made a molten calf to try and please rebellious tribes?

20. Name two of three people whom the Bible mentions as being mighty in strength and each killed a lion.

9. OLD TESTAMENT (1)

1. Following the death of Abel, Adam and Eve had another son. What was his name?
2. Why did God instruct Moses to make a bronze snake?
3. How many men did Gideon lead into battle against the Midianites?
4. Who was the father of Hophni and Phineas?
5. How was Elijah taken up to heaven?
6. Why did Elisha command the men of Jericho to put salt in a new bowl, which he then threw on a spring?
7. Who received permission from King Artaxerxes to re-build Jerusalem?
8. Which prophet wore a veil and why?
9. For whom did an angel prepare dinner?
10. Who prayed by an open window?

11. Which two persons were commanded to take off their shoes?

12. Who had a vision of a valley of dry bones?

13. Who proved themselves servants of the Lord by eating only vegetables and drinking only water?

14. Which prophetess played the tambourine?

15. Which city was saved from destruction by the repentence of its people?

16. Who was near to being killed by eating honey?

17. In whose reign was silver as plentiful as stones in Jerusalem?

18. When was a prayer offered from the depths of the sea?

19. Who was arrayed in purple with a gold chain around his neck?

20. Whose life was saved by listening to the warning of an angel?

10. OLD TESTAMENT (2)

1. Whose arms were held up by two people during a battle, causing victory for Israel's armies?
2. Which prophet put a yoke on his neck?
3. Which of the prophets was called from the plough?
4. What miracle occurred to enable a widow to pay off her debts?
5. What is the year of Jubilee mentioned in the Bible?
6. What was the last of the ten plagues in Egypt?
7. Which article of clothing was the token of a father's partiality?
8. How did Samson kill over 3000 people including himself?
9. Which sin is stated as having caused the destruction of Tyre?

10. Name one occasion when God sent sleep on individuals or people.

11. For how long did Moses' mother hide him?

12. For how long did the waters flood the earth during the time of Noah?

13. Who was Bathsheba's first husband?

14. Which king of Judah reigned for thirty-one years and was pleasing to the Lord?

15. To whom did the Ishmaelites sell Joseph?

16. What is the first of the ten commandments?

17. Who appeared before Joshua holding a sword?

18. Which angel appeared to Daniel while he was praying?

19. How long did it take Solomon to build the temple?

20. Who betrayed Samson to the Philistines?

11. NEW TESTAMENT (1)

1.   Who were the seven brothers who tried to drive out evil spirits by using the name of Jesus?

2.   At which place were magic books burned in public?

3.   Which prophet tied up his hands and feet with Paul's belt to illustrate Paul's future arrest?

4.   How old was Jesus when he began his public ministry?

5.   What was the first temptation experienced by Jesus when he went into the desert'?

6.   In the story of the Good Samaritan, in which direction was the traveller journeying?

7.   Apart from running, which sport does Paul use to illustrate his life as a Christian?

8.   How many times was Paul shipwrecked?

9.   To which Jewish tribe did Paul belong?

10. Whom does Paul urge to be a 'good soldier of Jesus Christ?'

11. In which New Testament book is a chapter devoted to 'faith'?

12. Which is the greatest and most important commandment?

13. When did the disciples think that Jesus was a ghost?

14. Jesus was seen talking to two men on the mountain where he was transfigured. Who were they?

15. Why had Barabbas been put into prison?

16. When Jesus died, what event occurred in the temple?

17. When Mary was pregnant and went to visit her cousin Elizabeth who was also expecting a child, how did Elizabeth respond to her greeting?

18. When Jesus healed a man born blind, which pool did he instruct the man to wash in?

19. Which ruler accused Paul of being mad?

20. Of faith, hope and love, which is the greatest?

12. NEW TESTAMENT (2)

1.　For what reason did Paul plead with Euodia and Syntyche?

2.　What are the fruits of the Spirit listed by Paul in Galatians?

3.　Who referred to the fact that he had a thorn in the flesh?

4.　How many times did he plead with the Lord to take away the thorn in the flesh?

5.　In Lystra when Paul healed a cripple, which gods did the people think that he and Barnabas were?

6.　Which woman had seven demons driven from her?

7.　Which pieces of armour does Paul refer to in Ephesians chapter six?

8.　At which hour did Peter preach on the Day of Pentecost?

9.　Name the three Marys who were present at Jesus's crucifixion.

10. What was the name of the field which Judas Iscariot bought with his reward for betraying Jesus?

11. To whom is the book of Acts addressed?

12. When Paul and Barnabas parted company, who were their new companions?

13. At Cenchrea, why did Paul have his hair cut off?

14. When Paul visited Ephesus why was there a riot?

15. Who, when cruelly put to death, prayed like his Lord for his murderers?

16. Which epistle did Paul write with his own hand?

17. On which occasion did Jesus state that he is the resurrection and the life?

18. Which church did Paul urge to stop incorporating ideas and philosophies from other religions with Christian truth?

19. Who refers to the tongue as being like the rudder of a ship?

20. Which articles used by Paul were taken to sick people who were then healed?

13. PLACES

1.   In which city was a forty day fast proclaimed?
2.   Where was Rachel buried?
3.   Where was an altar erected to 'the unknown god'?
4.   Where did Joshua set up twelve stones taken from the River Jordan?
5.   Which country was famed for its wisdom?
6.   What was the name of the promised land?
7.   Which was the ancient town famed for commerce?
8.   From which mountain did Jesus ascend into heaven?
9.   Upon which island did a snake fasten itself to Paul's hand?
10. Upon which road did the risen Jesus meet two of the disciples?

11. What is the name of the street where Paul received back his sight?

12. On which mountain was Moses given the ten commandments?

13. Where was Paul born?

14. Where did Jesus perform his first miracle?

15. From which city did Paul narrowly escape with his life?

16. Name the meeting place of a king and a witch.

17. In which river was Jesus baptised?

18. To which place did Jonah run away?

19. Into which sea were the plague of locusts swept?

20. On which mountains did Noah's ark come to rest?

14. WOMEN OF THE BIBLE (1)

1. Who was called 'a mother in Israel'?
2. Which queen saved her nation?
3. When King Ahaziah was put to death, what action was taken by his mother, Athaliah?
4. Which businesswoman did Paul baptise by the river at Philippi?
5. What were the names of Timothy's mother and grandmother?
6. Who was a holy woman, famed for works of love?
7. How did Abishai wish to kill King Saul?
8. Whose name means 'princess'?
9. Who 'gave her child to the Lord?'
10. Whose skin was suddenly covered with a dreaded disease and turned as white as snow?

11. To whom did Jesus first appear after his resurrection?

12. Who 'worshipped night and day, fasting and praying' in the temple?

13. What queen was a disobedient wife?

14. Six women took a journey which resulted in a royal wedding. Who was the bride?

15. Name one of two women whose ages are mentioned in the Bible.

16. How did Rahab aid the escape of the spies sent to Jericho?

17. Whose wife asked that her sons might sit on the right and left of Jesus in heaven?

18. What was Hadassah's other name?

19. Who were Naomi's daughters in law?

20. Who was the mother of Solomon?

15. WOMEN OF THE BIBLE (2)

1. Which queen sent a message under a false signature?
2. Who was Rachel's elder sister?
3. Who led armies into battle?
4. Who ridiculed a king for rejoicing and suffered for it?
5. What was the name of Moses' wife?
6. Why did the widow of Nain have cause to rejoice?
7. Which cast-out mother, in distress for want of water, threw her child under a bush to die?
8. Who was the only person to raise a voice against the mock trial and crucifixion of Jesus?
9. A shepherdess that Jacob met?
10. Which New Testament Jewess was a tentmaker?
11. When Peter escaped from prison, which servant answered the door of the house where he called?

12. Whose future husband was meditating in a field when he first met her?

13. For what reason was Caleb's daughter, Aesah, given to Othniel in marriage?

14. Who complained to Jesus that she'd been left to do all the work?

15. Whose daughter danced before King Herod, then demanded the head of John the Baptist in return?

16. Which queen visited King Solomon when she heard of his fame?

17. Who killed Sisera by driving a tent peg through his head?

18. Who did not die when a city's walls fell down?

19. What was Samson's mother told to avoid when she was pregnant?

20. Who held her place of judgement under a palm tree?

SECTION TWO

DISCOVERY!

DISCOVERY!

Answer the questions in each section and the first initials of each answer will join together to form a word.

ONE

1. The betrayer of Jesus.
2. The father of James.
3. The man who replaced the betrayer.
4. He was seen with another when Jesus was transfigured.
5. The apostle who was also called Peter.
       The initials will form the name of an apostle.

TWO

1. A prophet who ran away from God.
2. A name given to Jesus.
3. High Priest in the days of Saul and David.
4. An apostle called 'the Zealot.'
5. The wife of Elkanah.
       The initials will form the name of a boy king.

THREE

1. A woman who was always doing good.
2. Another word for 'father'.
3. The murdered owner of a vineyard.
4. A son of Jacob by Leah.
5. The second son of Joseph.
6. A flower mentioned in Luke's Gospel.

The initials form the name of a prophet.

FOUR

1. A New Testament Christian from Alexandria who was learned in the Scriptures.
2. A general whose leprosy was cleansed by Elisha.
3. A believer from Lystra who joined Paul on his second missionary journey.
4. The son of Saul who tried to succeed him as king.
5. A king of Israel.
6. Adam's first born.
7. The crowds cried this at Jesus' entry to Jerusalem.

The initials form the name of the place where people were first called Christians.

FIVE

1. One of the gifts brought to baby Jesus.
2. A prophet to Judah.
3. One of Job's friends.
4. A jewel of 'great price.'
5. The wife of Nabal.
6. A king of Tyre who helped David to build his palace.

The initials form the name of a place where Samuel prayed for, and judged Israel.

SIX

1. The archangel who appeared to Daniel.
2. A country celebrated for its gold and precious stones.
3. A Bible book which has holiness as its theme.
4. A son of Abraham.
5. A prophet who went to Paul and foretold a famine.
6. Paul wrote two epistles to this young church.
7. A musical instrument which was hung on the poplars.

The initials form the name of an awesome giant.

SEVEN

1. One of three who was thrown into a fiery furnace.
2. A pungent substance burned with the grain offering.
3. Cornelius was one.
4. An ancient city in Canaan given to Caleb.
5. A wicked king.
6. Jacob's father-in-law.

The initials form the name of a king's daughter.

EIGHT

1. A village where Jacob had a vision.
2. The home of the Joseph who buried Jesus in his family tomb.
3. A name given to the Lord.
4. The town in Galilee where Jesus grew up.
5. A friend of Paul who was seized by a mob.
6. A blind man healed by Jesus.
7. A son of Jacob.
8. A religious sect or party drawn largely from the priestly class.

The initials form the name of a companion of Paul.

NINE

1. David's father.
2. A city of Asia Minor where Paul preached, and which is mentioned in the book of Revelation.
3. A book of the Bible.
4. A prophet who was the son of Amoz.
5. It appeared like a pillar and guided the children of Israel.
6. A king of Judea who slew the children of Bethlehem.
7. A runaway slave.

The initials form the name of an ancient royal city.

TEN

1. A friend of Luke, and to whom two books of the Bible were written.
2. Eli's grandson who was born on the day of his death.
3. An apostle.
4. The original home of Abraham's family.
5. A place where the Jews met for worship.

The initials form the name of a book in the New Testament.

ELEVEN

1. There were ten in a parable of Jesus'.
2. A sacred wooden post possibly originally connected with tree worship.
3. A tree associated with a tax collector.
4. An epistle containing a famous chapter on faith.
5. A town on the shore of the Sea of Galilee.
6. The betrayer's second name.

The initials form the name of a disobedient queen.

TWELVE

1. A Jewish festival when the book of Esther is read.
2. The last book in the Bible.
3. Naomi's daughter in law who stayed behind.
4. This was offered to Christ on the cross as refreshment.
5. A beautiful garden.
6. A sign which was God's pledge that he would never flood the earth again.
7. An apostle.
8. The Queen of _ _ _ _ _ came to visit Solomon.

The initials form the name of a book containing wise sayings.

THIRTEEN

1. Another name for Jerusalem.
2. A Bible character whose name meant 'red'.
3. Thomas's other name.
4. A precious stone mentioned in the Bible.
5. A son of Ishmael.

The initials form the name of a priest.

FOURTEEN

1. A substance which Christians are called to be like.
2. The first letter of the Greek alphabet.
3. A parable mentions this seed.
4. A wicked queen.
5. A wife of Jacob.
6. Jacob's other name.
7. A capital city visited by Paul.

The initials form the capital of the northern kingdom of Israel in Bible times.

FIFTEEN

1. The first-born son of Joseph.
2. A tree mentioned in the Bible.

48

3.   One of the women who went to annoint Jesus' body following his death.
4.   The mother of Timothy.
5.   An animal cursed by God.

The initials form the name of a patriarch.

SIXTEEN

1.   An apostle.
2.   Abraham's wife.
3.   A tentmaker
4.   A monster mentioned in the book of Job.
5.   A high priest and king.
6.   A character famed for his immense strength.

The initials form the name of a book of poems.

SEVENTEEN

1.   A man who befriended Paul following his conversion.
2.   A slave girl who announced Peter's arrival following his escape from prison.
3.   One of Daniel's companions in exile who was also named Azariah.
4.   The first born of Jacob by Leah.

5. Saul's cousin and commander in chief of the army.
6. One of the 'seven churches of Asia' mentioned in Revelation.

The initials form the name of a mountain.

EIGHTEEN
1. The third son of David.
2. A salt sea.
3. A Hittite who was one of David's mighty warriors.
4. Paul's doctor companion.
5. The ancient name of Bethel named by Jacob after his ladder dream.
6. A prophet from Shiloh who protested against Solomon's idolatry.
7. The man who lived until he was 969 years old.

The initials reveal the name of a cave where a future king hid.

NINETEEN
1. The longest river in Palestine.
2. He hid one hundred prophets.
3. A venomous, clawed creature mentioned in the Bible.

4. 'God with us.'
5. A weapon mentioned in the Bible.
6. Eighth of the minor prophets.
   The initials form the name of a good king who
   honoured God.

TWENTY
1. A son born when his father was 100 years old.
2. A word used to describe the radiance, glory or presence of God dwelling in the midst of his people.
3. He stole silver, gold and clothing and his punishment was by stoning and cremation in the Vale of Achor.
4. The fifth son of Jacob and Leah.
5. The first man.
6. Sarah's handmaid.
   The initials form the name of a prophet.

TWENTY-ONE
1. Most famous collection of moral sayings of Christ.
2. Solomon's thone was inlaid with the product from this beast.
3. The church in Laodicea was this.

4. Another name for an animal which spoke to Balaam.
5. A measure of weight and money.

The initials form the name of Paul's companion on his second missionary journey.

TWENTY-TWO
1. The weapon that comes from Jesus' mouth in Revelation.
2. A goddess who brought business to craftsmen at Ephesus.
3. Paul had a vision of a man from this place.
4. The first king of Israel.
5. A substance used for annointing.
6. A son of Jacob.

The initials form the name of a strong man.

TWENTY-THREE
1. A prophetess who judged and delivered Israel.
2. A group of stargazers who could not interpret Nebuchadnezzar's dream.
3. Jesus said, 'I am the true _ _ _ _.'
4. God's description of himself when he met with

Moses by the burning bush.
5. The god of the Philistines.
    The initials form the name of a great king.

TWENTY-FOUR

1. The foolish husband of Abigail.
2. A man whom Paul commended in 2 Timothy as coming to his aid.
3. The father-in-law of a high priest.
4. A plant used for sprinkling blood.
    The initials form the name of a man of God.

TWENTY-FIVE

1. The evil wife of King Ahab.
2. A word which Jesus cried on the cross and which means 'my God.'
3. A collection of writings bearing on the Jewish law.
4. A son of Noah.
5. Isaac's wife.
6. The shortest of the minor prophets.
    The initials form the name of a father-in-law.

SECTION THREE

HIDDEN NAMES

1. BIBLE CHARACTERS

Each of the following sentences contain the name of a Bible character or characters, for example, in the sentence below, you will see that the hidden name is *'Eve'*.

The walk was long and *eve*ntful as two people sprained ankles, and one fell into a stream.

See how many you can find.

1.   Maria chose the smartest outfit she could find for her job interview the following day.

2.   Gina was delighted to find a rare antique plate at a market in her neighbouring town.

3.   Tom's ambition was to become the champion chess player in the local county tournament.

4.　The special agent quietly left the house, assured that all evidence of his search through the building had been removed.

5.　It was difficult to chose a present for Clive, but she at last found a belt to match his best pair of shoes.

6.　Tina was an excellent cook, and made sausage rolls and trifles to take to the party that night.

7.　Marian drew his attention to the leaking pipe and asked if he could repair it as soon as possible.

8.　The astrologer made a most exciting discovery while gazing at the stars through his new telescope.

9.　The young runaway wondered how long he could survive in this strange town without food or cash.

10.　Alan and Joan named their baby daughter Louise after her great grandmother.

2. BOOKS OF THE BIBLE

Find the names of books from the Bible hidden below.

1.   Giles is a creature of habit and always leaves the research laboratory at precisely five o'clock.

2.   Jane hated being delayed by a traffic jam, especially when she was already late for work.

3.   Donna hummed a tune as she set about her tasks in the greenhouse.

4.   The detective was making slow progress until he received an anonymous tip off.

5. Lisa went to the sales and chose a beautiful silk blouse to wear to the party that night.

6. Stuart bought a diesel car and was surprised to learn that it used less fuel than his previous model.

7. The monsters sharp, jagged teeth and awesome shape terrified her, and she ran for cover as it roared angrily.

8. The policeman investigating the case knew that some one had to be lying when the facts didn't make sense.

9. The jury listened to the evidence and concluded that the witness had not been truthful in his description of the events.

10. Carol prepared the games for the Christmas party while Jo baked a fruit cake.

3. BIBLE FOOD

Find the food hidden in the sentences below.

1. Doris knew he attributed his good looks to diet and exercise, and wished that she could be as enthusiastic about them.

2. Jim and Julie were good players and finished their game long before the other teams.

3. It was hard to tell that the two children were brother and sister as they differed greatly in personality and appearance.

4. The witness remembered that the victim had been given the watch one year earlier at his retirement presentation.

5.   The farmer had always planted cereal crops, but had decided upon growing rapeseed for a change that year.

6.   The scientist ushered his colleague into the lab, readjusted the microscope, and showed her his amazing discovery.

7.   Caleb uttered a loud cry when he discovered that his bicycle had been stolen.

8.   Dora is instructing people in several subjects at the local night school.

9.   Edward and Edgar licked their lips at the prospect of one of Mrs Bridges tasty stews.

10.   She was introduced to a man named Charles, then taken into another room for a detailed interview.

4. TREES IN THE BIBLE

Find the trees hidden in the sentences below.

1.   The red fire engine reached the scene within minutes, but the flames were by then out of control.

2.   Michael gave Jo a kite for her eighth birthday, and she flew it outside in the garden.

3.   It was difficult to stay calm on days when the director dropped into the office for a visit.

4.   She bought a blue lamp in exactly the same shade as her bedroom curtains.

5.   Joyce dared her friend to enter the competition and was delighted when she won.

SECTION FOUR

FILL THE GAPS

1. FILL THE GAPS
FAMOUS A's

The answers to the following questions begin with the letter 'A'. When you have found the answer, use your skill to fill in the gaps.

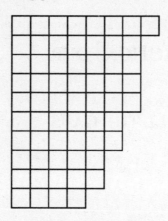

1   An Aramaic word meaning 'father'.
2   A companion of Daniel in exile.
3   The wife of Nabal, then David.
4   The son of Terah and husband of Sarah.
5   A valley near Jericho where Achan was executed.
6   A cave where David hid when pursued by Saul.
7   The first letter of the Greek alphabet.
8   A follower of Jesus who had befriended Paul after his conversion.
9   Noah's ark came to rest here.
10 A Greek city where Paul preached which was famous for its culture.

2. FILL THE GAPS
FAMOUS J's

The answers to all the following questions begin with the letter 'J'. When you have found the answer, use your skill to fill in the gaps.

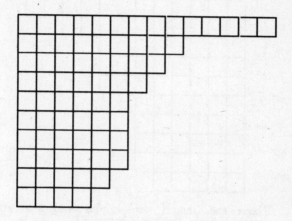

1 A wicked queen.
2 A New Testament epistle.
3 A ruler of the synagogue whose daughter was healed by Christ.
4 A prophet.
5 A famous city set in the hills of Judah.
6 The father of David.
7 Moses' father-in-law.
8 A river which flows into the lake of Galilee.
9 The son of Nun.
10 The son of Zechariah and Elizabeth.

3. FILL THE GAPS
FAMOUS P's

The answers to the following questions begin with the letter 'P'. When you have found the answer, use your skill to fill in the gaps.

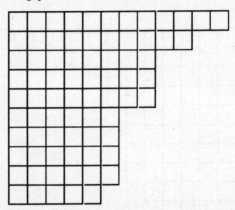

1 Hagar and Ishmael went to this wilderness after expulsion from Abraham's household.
2 The island to which the apostle John was banished.
3 The name given to the first five books of the Old Testament.
4 An epistle to the owner of a slave.
5 A high officer of Pharaoh to whom the Midianites sold Joseph.
6 David wrote seventy-three of them.
7 He led an Ethiopian eunuch to Christ.
8 A church mentioned in Revelation chapter three.
9 The place where Jacob wrestled with an angel.
10 A church brought into being on Paul's second missionary journey.

4. FILL THE GAPS
FAMOUS R's

The answers to the following questions begin with the letter 'R'. When you have found the answer, use your skill to fill in the gaps.

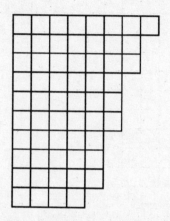

1   A word meaning 'great' and used for a person in a respected position.
2   The favourite wife of Jacob.
3   A sign of God's covenant with Noah.
4   The wife of Isaac.
5   A sea which divides north-east Africa from Arabia.
6   Jacob's first born by Leah.
7   A slave girl.
8   The wife of Boaz.
9   The birthplace and home of Saul.
10 A name given to Christ.

SECTION FIVE

LETTER AND NUMBER CODES

LETTER CODES

1. FOLLOWERS OF JESUS

De-code the different names by moving three letters to the right.

A B C D E F G H I J K L M N O P Q R S T U V W X Y Z

1 PFJLK MBQBO
2 GXJBP
3 GLEK
4 JXQQEBT
5 XKAOBT
6 MEFIFM
7 YXOQELIBJBT
8 QELJXP
9 GXJBP PLK LC XIMEBRP
10 GRAXP
11 QEXAABRP
12 JXOQEX
13 JXOV
14 IXWXORP
15 GLPBME LC XOFJXQEBX
16 JXOV JXDAXIBKB
17 GLXKKX
18 PQBMEBK
19 JXQQEFXP
20 WXZZEXBRP

LETTER CODES

2. NAMES OF GOD AND JESUS (1)

De-code the different names by moving three letters to the right.

A B C D E F G H I J K L M N O P Q R S T U V W X Y Z

1   YOBXA LC IFCB
2   ZEFBC ZLOKBOPQLKB
3   CFOPQ XKA IXPQ
4   DLA LC DILOV
5   DOBXQ EFDE MOFPQ
6   ELIV XKA QORB
7   HFKD LC MBXZB
8   IFDEQ LC QEB TLOIA
9   ILOA LC XII
10 JBPPFXE
11 JLOKFKD PQXO
12 JV CLOQOBPP
13 JV IXJM
14 LRO MLQQBO
15 MOBZFLRP PQRKB
16 OBCFKBO XKA MROFCFBO
17 PXKZQRXOV
18 PEBMEBOA
19 PROB CLRKAXQFLK
20 SFKB

3. NAMES OF GOD AND JESUS (2)

De-code the different names by moving three letters to the right.

A B C D E F G H I J K L M N O P Q R S T U V W X Y Z

1   TLOA LC IFCB
2   VLRO HBBMBO
3   PQOLKD QLTBO
4   PRK XKA PEFBIA
5   VLRO JXHBO
6   MOFKZB LC MBXZB
7   VLRO PEFBIA
8   OFDEQBLRP GRADB
9   IFLK LC GRAXE
10 ILOA LC ILOAP
11 ILOA DLA LC QORQE
12 FJXDB LC DLA
13 ELOK LC PXISXQFLK
14 CIXJB
15 EB TEL TFII ZLJB
16 BQBOKXI IFCB
17 XASLZXQB
18 ABIFSBOBO
19 ZOLTK LC DILOV
20 CXQEBO LC JBOZFBP

NUMBER CODES

4. JEWISH FESTIVALS/FASTS

Use the code table to unscramble the names of Jewish festivals and fasts.

1	2	3	4	5	6	7	8	9	10	11	12	13
A	B	C	D	E	F	G	H	I	J	K	L	M
14	15	16	17	18	19	20	21	22	23	24	25	26
N	O	P	Q	R	S	T	U	V	W	X	Y	Z

1   16, 21, 18, 9, 13
2   20, 1, 2, 5, 18, 14, 1, 3, 12, 5, 19
3   23,5,5,11,19
4   21,14,12,5,1,22,5,14,5,4   2,18,5,1,4
5   20,8,5   19,1,2,2,1,20,8
6   20,8,5   4,1,25   15,6   2,12,15,23,9,14,7   20
        18,21,13,16,5,20,19
7   20,8,5   4,1,25   15,6   1,20,15,14,5,13,5,14,20
8   6,5,19,20,9,22,1,12   15,6   12,9,7,8,20,19
9   6,1,19,20   15,6   19,5,22,5,14,20,5,5,14,20,8   15,6
        20,1,13,13,21,26
10   6,1,19,20   15,6   20,9,19,8,1,8   2,5 - 1,2
11   6,1,19.20   15,6   7,5,4,1,12,9,1,8
12   6,1,19,20   15,6   20,5,14,20,8   15,6   20,5,2,5,20
13   8,15,19,8,1,14,1,8   18,1,2,2,1
14   19,8,5,13,9,14,9   18,5,2,5,20
15   19,9,13,8,1,20   20,15,18,1,8

73

NUMBER CODES

5. PAUL's JOURNEYS

Use the code table below to unscramble names of places Paul visited.

1	2	3	4	5	6	7	8	9	10	11	12	13
A	B	C	D	E	F	G	H	I	J	K	L	M
14	15	16	17	18	19	20	21	22	23	24	25	26
N	O	P	Q	R	S	T	U	V	W	X	Y	Z

1   19,5,12,5,21,3,9,1
2   3,25,16,18,21,19
3   19,1,12,1,13,9,19
4   16,1,16,8,15,19
5   16,5,18,7,1
6   1,14,20,9,15,3,8
7   9,3,15,14,9,21,13
8   12,25,19,20,18,1
9   4,5,18,2,5
10   1,20,20,1,12,9,1
11   3,9,12,9,3,9,1
12   19,25,18,9,1
13   16,8,9,12,9,16,16,9
14   20,18,15,1,19
15   20,8,5,19,19,1,12,15,14,9,3,1
16   5,16,8,5,19,21,19
17   1,20,8,5,14,19
18   2,5,18,5,1
19   3,15,18,9,14,20,8
20   13,1,12,20,1

NUMBER CODES

6. PROPHETS AND PROPHETESSES

Use the code table below to unscramble names of prophets and prophetesses.

1	2	3	4	5	6	7	8	9	10	11	12	13
A	B	C	D	E	F	G	H	I	J	K	L	M

14	15	16	17	18	19	20	21	22	23	24	25	26
N	O	P	Q	R	S	T	U	V	W	X	Y	Z

1   1,2,18,1,8,1,13
2   10,15,5,12
3   10,15,14,1,8
4   9,19,1,9,1,8
5   13,9,3,1,8
6   10,5,18,5,13,9,1,8
7   5,26,5,11,9,5,12
8   13,1,12,1,3,8,9
9   4,1,14,9,5,12
10 14,1,8,21,13
11 8,15,19,5,1
12 1,13,15,19
13 8,1,7,7,1,9
14 15,2,1,4,9,1,8
15 8,1,2,1,11,11,21,11
16 26,5,3,8,1,18,9,1,8
17 5,12,9,10,1,8
18 4,5,2,15,18,1,8
19 5,12,9,19,8,1
20 8,21,12,4,1,8

75

NUMBER CODES

7. RIVERS, WATERWAYS, SEAS AND LAKES

Use the code table below to unscramble the names of rivers, seas and lakes.

1	2	3	4	5	6	7	8	9	10	11	12	13
A	B	C	D	E	F	G	H	I	J	K	L	M
14	15	16	17	18	19	20	21	22	23	24	25	26
N	O	P	Q	R	S	T	U	V	W	X	Y	Z

1   10,15,18,4,1,14
2   20,1,12,9,12,5,5
3   4,5,1,4   19,5,1
4   14,9,12,5
5   5,21,16,8,18,1,20,5,19
6   18,5,4   19,5,1
7   20,9,2,5,18,9,1,19
8   20,9,7,18,9,19
9   7,18,5,1,20   19,5,1
10   13,1,18,1,8
11   3,8,9,14,14,5,18,5,20,8
12   1,2,1,14,1
13   13,5,14,26,1,12,5,8
14   12,1,11,5   20,9,13,19,1,8
15   7,9,8,15,14
16   16,8,1,18,16,1,18
17   11,9,19,8,15,14
18   10,1,2,2,15,11
19   1,18,14,15,14
20   11,1,14,1,8

76

NUMBER CODES

8. VALLEYS IN THE BIBLE

Use the code table below to unscramble names of valleys.

1	2	3	4	5	6	7	8	9	10	11	12	13
A	B	C	D	E	F	G	H	I	J	K	L	M
14	15	16	17	18	19	20	21	22	23	24	25	26
N	O	P	Q	R	S	T	U	V	W	X	Y	Z

1   1,3,8,15,18
2   1,9,10,1,12,15,14
3   2,1,3,1
4   2,5,18,1,3,1,8
5   5,12,1,8
6   19,9,4,4,9,13
7   8,9,14,14,15,13
8   9,16,8,20,1,20,5,12
9   11,9,14,7,19
10 12,5,2,1,14,15,14
11 18,5,16,8,1,9,13
12 19,1,12,20
13 19,15,18,5,11
14 10,5,8,15,19,8,1,16,8,1,20
15 1,18,14,15,14
16 19,8,1,22,5,8
17 5,19,4,18,1,5,12,15,14
18 19,8,5,16,8,5,12,1,8
19 19,9,12,15,1,13
20 20,25,18,15,16,15,5,15,14

77

SECTION SIX

ANAGRAMS

1. BIRDS IN THE BIBLE

1	WHKA	11	CRANTOMOR
2	LLAWOSW	12	LLGU
3	SWARORP	13	NEROH
4	LOW	14	LQAIU
5	KROST	15	DAEGITRPR
6	LEGAE	16	CHRISOT
7	RUVTELU	17	VEOD
8	NRAEV	18	NPGOEI
9	IKET	19	HUSTRH
10	SORPEY	20	TISFW

2. ANIMALS IN THE BIBLE

1	LUME	11	SAS
2	AMLCE	12	GSIP
3	ATOG	13	YENDOK
4	OILN	14	EHSEP
5	RODEPAL	15	ARBE
6	FLOW	16	XFO
7	RAHE	17	MELO
8	EWLASE	18	SUEMO
9	DREE	19	WAHEL
10	SHERO	20	LRADIZ

3. PLANTS, HERBS AND SPICES IN THE BIBLE

1	TIMN	11	TASTEC
2	LIDL	12	ANYOCH
3	MIUCN	13	FASORNF
4	ERU	14	SPYOSH
5	DRECIARON	15	DEMAKANR
6	RATUDSM	16	LYIL
7	SMULACA	17	LAGNAMUB
8	NANOMICN	18	NANFIKCNERES
9	KENDARPSI	19	SINAE
10	DORWOMOW	20	LOMAWL

4. FOOD IN THE BIBLE

Unscramble the following anagrams to reveal different food mentioned in the Bible.

1	MERGOTEAPAN	11	SANBE
2	SEGARP	12	IGRACL
3	ESECEH	13	PTSLE
4	ERBAYL	14	EBTTRU
5	LISTENL	15	LNAMDOS
6	CERBUMUC	16	OYNHE
7	LAPEP	17	ISANIRS
8	LIMELT	18	HIFS
9	NOSNIO	19	KELE
10	MENOL	20	GFI

81

5. PRECIOUS AND SEMI-PRECIOUS STONES

1	DONIMAD	10	BURY
2	LEDERMA	11	TALCSYR
3	PARSEJ	12	ETAAG
4	PHEASIPR	13	LANICRAEN
5	LARPE	14	OLYLEW RATZUQ
6	NXOY	15	ZOPTA
7	HONDYLCACE	16	QOURSTIEU
8	STEAMYHT	17	TRANGE
9	LYREB		

6. KINGS IN THE BIBLE

1	HISAJO	11	AMOROJEB
2	VIDAD	12	ATMOJH
3	HABA	13	AZAH
4	MORBEAHO	14	EHZHRACIH
5	LONSMOO	15	KEIAHZEH
6	ZAMIAHA	16	SHEMSANA
7	SAJHEOH	17	AEJZOHAH
8	UEHJ	18	JOTESAHPHAH
9	IHAAZHA	19	AEBAZRZLSH
10	SHOJA	20	SARXTAXREE

7. MOUNTAINS AND HILLS OF THE BIBLE

1 MAPIHER
2 SIVLOE
3 ATRARA
4 HIROMA
5 NOZI
6 BONE
7 ALBIGO
8 NEMORH
9 ROHBE
10 LABE
11 MACLER
12 INISA
13 ZEGMIRI
14 NARPA
15 ALDIGE
16 ALAHAB
17 HORME
18 RAIMAB
19 ROH
20 ROTBA

SECTION SEVEN

HIDDEN WORDS

HIDDEN WORDS

1. PENTECOST

When Peter preached on the day of Pentecost, people from many places heard his message. Find the names of these areas hidden below.

M	O	P	A	M	A	S	O	C	H	E
A	P	S	Y	E	I	U	B	A	Y	L
L	I	A	G	S	G	T	E	P	U	I
A	D	Y	M	O	Y	N	A	P	P	A
A	P	J	C	P	R	O	H	A	A	S
T	I	U	T	o	H	P	W	D	R	I
U	E	D	B	T	P	Y	Y	O	T	G
S	T	A	E	A	B	E	L	C	H	Y
P	E	E	L	M	O	Z	L	I	I	P
A	R	A	B	I	A	D	E	A	A	N
A	C	Y	T	A	Y	B	I	L	M	O

Parthia	Media	Elam	Mesopotamia
Judaea	Cappadocia	Pontus	Asia
Phrygia	Pamphylia	Egypt	Crete
Libya	Arabia		

86

HIDDEN WORDS

2. THE TRIBES OF ISRAEL

Find the names of the tribes of Israel hidden below. They are hidden diagonally, horizontally, vertically and backwards.

L	A	E	N	D	A	R	H	R	I
I	M	O	B	A	W	A	E	H	E
L	D	A	E	Z	D	H	L	T	P
A	T	Y	N	U	S	C	H	S	H
T	S	G	J	A	B	A	N	E	R
H	O	I	A	M	S	S	I	E	A
P	U	V	M	D	T	S	V	K	I
A	W	E	I	E	S	I	E	J	M
N	G	L	N	T	O	V	I	H	O
F	R	E	U	B	E	N	S	A	B

Reuben   Gad   Manasseh   Levi
Judah   Ephraim   Asher   Issachar
Dan   Simeon   Benjamin   Naphtali

HIDDEN WORDS
3. GOD'S NAMES

Find the names hidden below.

P	A	X	H	S	A	B	A	O	T	H	U
O	B	S	A	K	E	H	P	O	R	Z	R
L	A	H	M	O	K	U	V	L	T	N	T
T	H	U	M	L	C	N	A	S	B	C	Z
A	R	B	A	T	I	Y	I	H	A	D	A
M	E	K	H	S	I	D	D	A	K	E	M
O	I	J	S	H	K	E	T	L	E	C	U
T	C	I	O	E	H	L	A	O	H	F	Q
W	A	R	N	R	I	O	G	M	O	T	S
C	T	U	O	I	P	H	E	A	L	L	N
F	R	A	U	J	N	A	W	I	E	H	J
L	O	S	D	E	L	Y	O	N	Y	B	I

Jehovah ......
   ... Ropheka (The Lord Your Healer)
   ... Mekaddishkem (The Lord Our Sanctifier)
   ... Tsidkenu (The Lord Our Righteousness)
   ... Shammah (The Lord is There)
   ... Shalom (The Lord Our Peace)
   ... Eloheka (The Lord Your God)
   ... Nissi (The Lord My Banner)
   ... Rohi (The Lord My Shepherd)
   ... Jireh (The Lord My Provider)
   ... Elohay (The Lord My God)
   ... Sabaoth (The Lord of Hosts)

88

HIDDEN WORDS

4. JEWISH MONTHS

Find the names of Jewish months hidden below. They are hidden diagonally, horizontally, vertically and backwards.

M	T	H	T	E	B	E	T	J	M
M	E	T	A	B	E	H	S	A	K
Y	A	L	F	A	D	A	R	E	E
V	D	B	U	Y	N	C	A	T	O
H	N	O	T	L	H	S	Y	A	S
I	T	I	I	E	Y	I	Y	M	H
C	H	I	S	L	E	V	I	M	E
B	A	V	H	A	B	A	N	U	Z
A	A	H	R	B	N	N	L	Z	O
N	N	O	I	S	I	H	T	D	A

Nisan	Iyyar	Sivan	Tammuz
Ab	Elul	Tishri	Marchesvan
Chislev	Tebeth	Shebat	Adar

89

HIDDEN WORDS

5. GATES IN THE BIBLE

Find the names of gates below

O	N	O	E	P	H	R	A	I	M
T	I	B	L	S	T	S	A	E	B
Y	A	J	E	D	R	A	I	T	E
E	T	R	E	N	R	O	C	F	L
L	N	O	X	Q	J	K	H	W	D
L	U	F	I	T	U	A	E	B	D
A	O	R	E	T	S	U	M	Z	I
V	F	U	D	A	K	H	P	I	M
W	A	T	E	R	H	T	R	O	N
L	H	T	A	N	N	E	G	N	W
A	S	H	E	E	P	G	N	U	D

Benjamin	Beautiful	Ephraim	Gennath
Zion	Dung	Water	Sheep
Valley	North	Fish	Fountain
Corner	Horse	Muster	Miphkad
Middle	Old	East	

90

6. OLD TESTAMENT CHARACTERS

Find the names of Old Testament Characters in the Bible hidden below. They are hidden diagonally, backwards, horizontally and vertically.

A	B	I	G	A	I	L	S	O	D	L
H	L	E	J	O	S	E	P	H	K	E
A	O	S	I	O	T	D	A	T	L	U
Z	H	T	S	H	N	N	A	I	E	M
N	A	H	T	A	N	A	J	V	V	A
B	O	E	X	A	U	A	H	A	I	S
O	N	R	H	R	H	L	A	S	E	D
A	H	A	M	O	P	D	Z	H	V	F
Z	B	I	S	N	A	O	C	T	E	K
H	T	U	R	M	A	I	R	I	M	S
A	N	L	A	U	H	S	O	J	F	G

Abigail	Nathan	Noah	Joseph
Jonah	Samuel	Joshua	Ham
Seth	Ahaz	Ruth	Hannah
Aaron	Boaz	Saul	David
Adam	Esther	Levi	Miriam

7. PLACES IN THE BIBLE

Find the names of places in the Bible hidden below. They are hidden diagonally, backwards, horizontally and vertically.

H	C	O	I	T	N	A	M	S	L	E	D
I	S	A	O	R	T	Y	A	S	P	E	P
N	P	J	J	H	R	M	U	H	B	U	O
J	U	D	E	A	A	R	E	E	L	T	X
O	G	N	R	R	P	S	R	O	M	E	S
L	S	C	I	Y	U	E	O	L	M	L	I
E	D	A	C	S	A	S	Y	M	J	I	D
H	E	N	H	T	C	S	A	O	T	M	O
T	R	A	O	Y	T	U	P	L	O	A	N
E	B	A	D	R	S	P	L	A	E	C	P
B	E	N	A	E	A	S	B	Q	R	M	A
A	L	E	J	M	U	I	N	O	C	I	C

Athens	Ephesus	Patmos	Miletus
Bethel	Cyprus	Joppa	Lystra
Troas	Myra	Sidon	Canaan
Jerusalem	Emmaus	Samaria	Jericho
Iconium	Berea	Rome	Judea
Moab	Tyre	Antioch	

8. WOMEN OF THE BIBLE

Find the names of women in the Bible hidden below. They are hidden diagonally, backwards, horizontally and vertically.

S	B	E	R	N	I	C	E	L	I	D	H
T	Y	A	L	O	I	S	M	R	T	C	A
X	O	N	E	I	H	L	A	E	H	E	L
N	R	U	T	H	Z	E	R	H	S	B	L
R	A	I	D	Y	L	A	Y	T	A	E	I
M	H	O	T	A	C	J	B	S	V	O	Z
S	A	C	M	H	O	H	T	E	I	H	M
O	B	R	E	I	H	A	E	L	T	P	E
F	O	L	T	I	H	A	N	N	A	H	O
S	A	R	A	H	J	T	G	O	R	E	L
D	E	B	O	R	A	H	D	A	O	T	H
H	T	A	L	L	I	C	S	I	R	P	C

Zillah	Priscilla	Mary	Syntyche
Elizabeth	Jael	Ruth	Martha
Deborah	Phoebe	Esther	Chloe
Bernice	Eve	Lydia	Rachel
Leah	Hannah	Rahab	Hagar
Sarah	Vashti	Lois	

9. NEW TESTAMENT CHARACTERS

Find the names of New Testament Characters in the Bible hidden below. They are hidden diagonally, backwards, horizontally and vertically.

A	T	H	N	E	H	P	E	T	S	L	O
T	I	M	O	T	H	Y	U	R	M	E	I
E	T	A	D	M	R	E	T	E	P	K	H
U	U	T	E	A	I	D	Y	L	J	U	P
N	S	T	M	R	T	A	C	O	C	L	E
I	C	H	A	T	H	U	H	H	O	R	S
C	A	E	S	H	O	N	U	I	L	M	O
E	L	W	J	A	M	E	S	E	A	O	J
N	O	M	I	S	A	J	V	R	Z	Y	E
J	A	I	R	U	S	I	K	E	D	U	J
O	R	D	S	A	B	A	N	R	A	B	U
X	S	U	M	I	H	P	O	R	T	G	A

Matthew	Eutychus	Lydia	John
Martha	Chloe	Thomas	Mark
Stephen	Demas	Joseph	Eunice
Titus	Peter	Lois	Mary
Luke	James	Timothy	Levi
Jairus	Simon	Barnabas	Jude
Trophimus			

94

SECTION EIGHT

PAIRS

PAIRS

Link the following pairs:

Abraham	Rebekah
Aquila	Ruth
Isaac	Eve
Boaz	Elizabeth
David	Jochebed
Moses	Sarah
Jacob	Bathsheba
Adam	Leah
Amram	Priscilla
Zechariah	Zipporah

* * * * * *

Ananias	Rachel
Ahab	Elisheba
Jacob	Delilah
Aaron	Jezebel
Chuza	Sapphira
Joseph	Hannah
Ahasuerus	Naomi
Samson	Asenath
Elkanah	Esther
Elimelech	Joanna

PAIRS

Link the following pairs:

James	Mary
Martha	Jonathon
Rachel	Abel
David	Caleb
Esau	John
Cain	Elisha
Peter	Leah
Philip	Andrew
Elijah	Isaac
Joshua	Herodias

* * * * * *

Hagar	Timothy
Hannah	Solomon
Elizabeth	Ishmael
Eunice	King Ahaziah
Sarah	Jesus
Ruth	Samuel
Bathsheba	Jacob
Rachel	Joseph
Athaliah	John the Baptist
Mary	Obed

PAIRS

Link the following pairs:

Cain	Phinehas
Eli	Enosh
Noah	Rehoboam
Seth	Enoch
Saul	Jonathon
Nun	Gideon
Zebedee	Shem
Solomon	Abijah
Jeroboam	James
Joash	Joshua

* * * * * *

Hosea	Jehosheba
Lappidoth	Gomer
Silas	Jambres
Jehoida	The Tax Collector
Jannes	Paul
Felix	The Whale
Agrippa	Deborah
Sodom	Bernice
The Pharisee	Gomorrah
Jonah	Drusilla

ANSWERS

SECTION 1: QUIZZES

1 GENERAL KNOWLEDGE (1)

1. Cypress wood - Genesis 6:14
2. Fig tree - Matthew 21:19
3. Omega - Revelation 22:13
4. Ebenezer - 1 Samuel 7:12
5. Laodicea - Revelation 3:14-22
6. Jonathan's son Mephibosheth - 2 Samuel 4:4
7. Hosea - Hosea 1:2
8. Genesis and Revelation - Genesis 2:9, Revelation 22:1-2
9. Methuselah - Genesis 5:27
10. The river Nile turned to blood - Exodus 7:20
11. They were giants - Numbers 13:33
12. Sodom and Gomorrah - Deuteronomy 29:23
13. 17 - Genesis 37:2
14. He didn't believe the angel who told him that a son would be born to his wife and himself.
15. Matthias - Acts 1:23-26
16. Jairus's daughter - Matthew 9:25, Widow of Nain's son - Luke 7:15, Lazarus - John 11:44
17. Acts 22
18. At the stoning of Stephen - Acts 7:58
19. The Apostle John - John 21:25
20. Twice. At the beginning of his ministry - John 2:14,16 and near its close - Matthew 21:12-13

2 GENERAL KNOWLEDGE (2)

1. Jesus - John 19:23.
2. Mara, which means bitter. She said that she went

100

away full and came back empty. She said that the Lord had brought misfortune upon her. - Ruth 1:20-21

3.   Nebuchadnezzar, King of Babylon - Jeremiah 25:9

4.   150.

5.   His mantle - 2 Kings 2:13

6.   Barnabas - Acts 13:2

7.   Rubies - Proverbs 31:10

8.   Daniel - Daniel 10:1

9.   Honour your mother and father - Exodus 20:12

10.   They were instructed to take a branch of hyssop, dip it in the blood of the Passover lamb and paint some on the door frame. - Exodus 12:22

11.   King Solomon sent for them for the purpose of building the temple - 2 Chronicles 2:8

12.   John's baptism was the baptism of repentence and Jesus's was the baptism of the Holy Spirit - Mark 1:4-8

13.   The Sea of Tiberias - John 21:1

14.   They were told to go and show themselves to the priests - Luke 17:14

15.   The Pastoral Epistles - because they contain Paul's advice to two young pastors.

16.   Bethany - Matthew 26:6

17.   Job's comforters - Job 42:9

18.   Every day except the Sabbath - Exodus 16:26

19.   At Lazarus's grave - John 11:35, Over Jerusalem - Luke 19:41, In Gethsemane - Hebrews 5:7.

20.   Naboth - 1 Kings 21.

3   INITIALS (1)

1.   Felix - Acts 23:24, Festus - Acts 24:27, Fortunatus - 1 Corinthians 16:17

2. Peniel - Genesis 32:31
3. Bethesda - John 5:1-11
4. The tower of Babel - Genesis 11:1-9
5. Artemis - Acts 19:23-24
6. Levi - Luke 5:28
7. Mount Moriah - 2 Chronicles 3:1
8. Zadok - 1 Chronicles 29:23
9. Gamaliel - Acts 5:34
10. Obed - Ruth 4:21
11. Gerasenes - Luke 8:26
12. Purim - Esther 9:26
13. Naaman - 2 Kings 5
14. Dagon - 1 Samuel 5:2
15. Ichabod - 1 Samuel 4:21
16. Shiloh - 1 Samuel 4:4
17. Cephas - John 1:42
18. Patmos - Revelation 1:9
19. Mordecai - Esther 2:5-7
20. Ur - Genesis 15:7

4 INITIALS (2)
1. Feast of Tabernacles - Leviticus 23:33-43
2. Zoar - Genesis 19:23
3. Meribah - Numbers 20:11-13
4. Adullam - 1 Samuel 22:1
5. Jericho - 2 Chronicles 28:15
6. Solomon - 1 Chronicles 22:9
7. Josiah - 2 Chronicles 34:1
8. Tamar - 2 Samuel 13:1
9. Moab - Ruth 1:1
10. Levi - Deuteronomy 18:1
11. Nebo - Deuteronomy 32:49-50

12. Dan - Joshua 19:40
13. Baal - Judges 3:7
14. Philemon
15. Melchizedek - Hebrews 7:1
16. Phoebe - Romans 16:1
17. Xerxes - Esther 2:16-17
18. Ham - Genesis 5:32
19. Uz - Job 1:1
20. Joseph - Acts 4:36

5 MEN OF THE BIBLE (1)

1. Elijah - Luke 9:30-33
2. Mark - Colossians 4:10
3. Caleb - Numbers 14:22-24
4. Gideon - Judges 6:11
5. Joshua - Joshua 10:12-13
6. Saul - 1 Samuel 31:4
7. Abel - Genesis 4:8
8. John - Revelation 1:4
9. Stephen - Acts 7:59
10. Elisha - 2 Kings 4:34
11. Darius the Mede - Daniel 5:30; 6:1-28
12. Moses - Exodus 18:1
13. Caesar Augustus - Luke 2:1
14. Aaron - Numbers 17:8
15. Haman - Esther 7:10
16. Daniel - 1 Chronicles 3:1
17. Judas Iscariot - Matthew 26:24
18. Caiaphas - Matthew 26:57
19. Esau- Genesis 25:25
20. Lazarus - John 11:1-2

6   MEN OF THE BIBLE (2)

1.   The Ethiopian eunuch - Acts 8:26-39
2.   Peter - Acts 12:8
3.   Nicodemus - John 3:2
4.   David - 1 Samuel 21:12-13
5.   Samson - Judges 15:15
6.   Timothy - 1 Timothy 1:2
7.   Onesimus - Philemon:10-15
8.   Amos - Amos 1:1
9.   Isaac - because Sarah said that God had brought her laughter in her old age and everyone who heard about it would laugh with her - Genesis 21:4-6
10. Obadiah - 1 Kings 18:4
11. Abraham - Genesis 18:1-8
12. Enoch - Hebrews 11:15
13. Barnabas - Acts 4:36
14. Nebuchadnezzar - Daniel 4:33
15. Ananias - Acts 9:9-18
16. James - Acts 12:2
17. He fell asleep and fell from a third storey window - Acts 20:9-12
18. Cornelius - Acts 10:5
19. Simon of Cyrene - Mark 15:21
20. Aristarchus - Acts 27:2

7   PROFESSIONS

1.   Paul, Priscilla and Aquila - Acts 18:3
2.   Zaccheus - Luke 19:2 and Matthew - Matthew 9:9
3.   Amos 7:14
4.   Tertullus - Acts 24:1 or Zenas - Titus 3:13
5.   Ishmael - Genesis 21:18-20
6.   Esau - Genesis 25:27-28

7. Deborah, Rebekah's nurse - Genesis 35:8
8. Uzziah - 2 Chronicles 26:10
9. Samuel - 1 Samuel 7:15-16
10. Nimrod - Genesis 10:8-9
11. Jubal - Genesis 4:21
12. Simon - Acts 9:43
13. Cornelius - Acts 10:27-33
14. Lydia, a seller of purple - Acts 16:13-14
15. Demetrius - Acts 19:24
16. Philip (Acts 21:8-9)
17. Rahab - Joshua 2:1
18. Simon, Andrew, James, John (Matt 4:18-22)
19. Adam (Genesis 2:15)
20. Nehemiah (Nehemiah 1:11)

8 ANIMALS AND BIRDS

1. Balaam's ass - Numbers 22:28
2. A lion - 1 Kings 13:24
3. Turtle dove, pigeon - Leviticus 5:7
4. Camels - Job 1:3
5. Foxes - Judges 15: 4-6
6. The eagle - 2 Samuel 1:23
7. Solomon - 1 Kings 10:22
8. Bears - 2 Kings 2:24
9. Ravens fed Elijah - 1 Kings 17:3-6
10. Jeremiah - Jeremiah 13:23
11. David - 2 Samuel 22:34
12. The leopard - Isaiah 11:6
13. Frogs - Exodus 8:5-6
14. A lamb or a kid - Exodus 12:5
15. A bull - 1 Kings 18:33
16. Rams horns - Joshua 6:4

17. Locusts and honey - Matthew 3:4
18. Job - Job 39:13,14
19. Aaron - Exodus 32:22-24
20. Samson - Judges 14:5, David - 1 Samuel 17:34, Benaiah - 2 Samuel 23:20

9 OLD TESTAMENT (1)

1. Seth - Genesis 4:25
2. When people were bitten by poisonous snakes they had only to look to the bronze snake to be healed - Numbers 21:9
3. Three hundred - Judges 7:7
4. Eli - 1 Samuel 1:3
5. He was taken up in a whirlwind on a chariot of fire with horses of fire - 2 Kings 2:11
6. The water was not pure, making the land unproductive - 2 Kings 2:19-22
7. Nehemiah - Nehemiah 2:5-6
8. Moses wore a veil because his face shone so brightly when he had been in the presence of the Lord - Exodus 34:33
9. Elijah - 1 Kings 19:4-8
10. Daniel - Daniel 6:10
11. Moses and Joshua - Exodus 3:5, Joshua 5:13-15
12. Ezekiel - Ezekiel 37
13. Daniel, Shadrach, Meshach and Abednego - Daniel 1:6,16
14. Miriam - Exodus 15:20
15. Ninevah - Jonah 3:4-10
16. Jonathan - 1 Samuel 14:24-27,43,45
17. Solomon's - 1 Kings 10:27
18. When Jonah was in the whale - Jonah 2:1

19. Daniel - Daniel 5:7,16,29
20. Lot - Genesis 19:15

10 OLD TESTAMENT (2)
1. Moses' arms - Exodus 17:9-13
2. Jeremiah - Jeremiah 27:2
3. Elisha - 1 Kings 19:19-20
4. Her olive oil multiplied - 2 Kings 4:4-7
5. The fiftieth year - Leviticus 25:8-54
6. Death of the first born - Exodus 11:5
7. A coat of many colours - Genesis 37:3
8. By pushing two pillars which held up a building and causing it to collapse - Judges 16:27-30
9. The Prince of Tyre had become proud and set himself up as God - Ezekiel 28:2
10. Adam - Genesis 2:21, Abraham - Genesis 15:12, Saul and his army - 1 Samuel 26:12
11. Three months - Exodus 2:2
12. 150 days - Genesis 7:24
13. Uriah - 2 Samuel 11:3
14. Josiah - 2 Chronicles 34:1-2
15. Potiphar - Genesis 39:1
16. Worship no other god - Exodus 20:3
17. An angel, the commander of the Lord's army - Joshua 5:13-14
18. Gabriel - Daniel 9:21
19. Twenty years - 2 Chronicles 8:1
20. Delilah - Judges 16:18-21

11 NEW TESTAMENT (1)
1. The sons of Sceva - Acts 19:11-17
2. Ephesus - Acts 19:19

3.   Agabus - Acts 21:10-11

4.   Thirty - Luke 3:23

5.   Satan tempted him to turn stones into bread - Luke 4:3; Matt 4:2

6.   From Jerusalem to Jericho - Luke 10:30

7.   Boxing - 1 Corinthians 9:26

8.   Three times - 2 Corinthians 11:25

9.   The tribe of Benjamin - Philippians 3:5

10. Timothy - 2 Timothy 2:3

11. Hebrews 11

12. Love the Lord your God with all your heart and with all your soul and with all your mind - Matthew 22:37

13. When he walked on the water - Mark 6:49

14. Elijah and Moses - Mark 9:4

15. He had taken part in a riot and a murder - Luke 23:19

16. The curtain in the temple was torn in two from top to bottom - Mark 15:38

17. Elizabeth's baby jumped with gladness - Luke 1:44

18. The Pool of Siloam - John 9:7

19. Festus - Acts 26:24

20. Love - 1 Corinthians 13:13

12   NEW TESTAMENT (2)

1.   They had squabbled and he was pleading with them to sort out their differences - Philippians 4:2

2.   Love, joy, peace, patience, kindness, goodness, faithfulness, gentleness, self-control - Galatians 5:22

3.   Paul - 2 Corinthians 12:7

4.   Three times - 2 Corinthians 12:8

5.   They thought that Barnabas was Zeus and Paul

Hermes - Acts 14:12

6. Mary Magdalene - Mark 16:9

7. The belt of truth, breastplate of righteousness, feet fitted with readiness that comes from the gospel of peace, shield of faith, helmet of salvation, sword of the Spirit - Ephesians 6:14-17

8. Nine o'clock - Acts 2:15

9. Mary the mother of Jesus, Mary Magdalene and Mary the wife of Clopas - John 19:25

10. Akeldema - the field of blood - Acts 1:19

11. Theophilus - Acts 1:1

12. Barnabas took John Mark and Paul was accompanied by Silas - Acts 15:39-40

13. He had taken a vow - Acts 18:18

14. The silversmiths thought that if many people were converted they would stop worshipping the goddess Artemis and would no longer buy their craftwares made in her likeness - Acts 19:23-29

15. Stephen - Acts 7:60

16. The letter to the Galatians - Galatians 6:11

17. On the occasion following the death of Lazarus - John 11:25

18. The church at Colossae - Colossians 2:8

19. James - James 3:4-6

20. Handkerchiefs and aprons - Acts 19:12

13 PLACES

1. Nineveh - Jonah 3:5

2. Bethlehem - Genesis 35:19-20

3. Athens - Acts 17:23

4. Gilgal - Joshua 4:19-23

5. Egypt - 1 Kings 4:30

6. Canaan
7. Tyre - Isaiah 23:3
8. Mount of Olives - Acts 1:12
9. Malta - Acts 28:1
10. The road to Emmaus - Luke 24:13
11. Straight Street - Acts 9:11-18
12. Sinai - Exodus 19:20
13. Tarsus of Cilicia - Acts 22:3
14. Cana in Galilee - John 2:1-11
15. Damascus - 2 Corinthians 11:32
16. Endor - 1 Samuel 28:7-8
17. River Jordan - Matthew 3:13
18. Tarshish - Jonah 1:3
19. The Red Sea - Exodus 10:19
20. Ararat - Genesis 8:4

14 WOMEN OF THE BIBLE (1)

1. Deborah - Judges 5:7
2. Esther - Esther 8:3
3. She had the royal family of the house of Judah destroyed and made herself queen - 2 Chronicles 22:10
4. Lydia - Acts 16:14-15
5. Eunice and Lois - 2 Timothy 1:5
6. Dorcas, also named Tabitha - Acts 9:36
7. By plunging a spear through him - 1 Samuel 26:8
8. Sarah - Genesis 17:15
9. Hannah - 1 Samuel 1:23,28
10. Miriam - Numbers 12:10
11. Mary Magdalene - Mark 16:9
12. Anna the prophetess - Luke 2:36
13. Queen Vashti - Esther 1:12
14: Abigail - 1 Samuel 25:42

15: Sarah (127) - Genesis 23:1, Anna (84) - Luke 2:36
16. She covered them with stalks of flax, then let them down through the window with a cord - Joshua 2:6,15
17. Zebedee's wife (Salome) - Matthew 20:20-21
18. Esther - Esther 2:7
19. Ruth and Orpah - Ruth 1:4
20. Bathsheba - 1 Kings 2:13

15 WOMEN OF THE BIBLE (2)
1. Jezebel used Ahab's name - 1 Kings 21:8
2. Leah - Genesis 29:16
3. Deborah - Judges 4:9
4. Michal - 2 Samuel 6:20-23
5. Zipporah - Exodus 2:21
6. Jesus raised her son from the dead - Luke 7:11-15
7. Hagar - Genesis 21:15,16
8. Pilate's wife - Matthew 27:19
9. Rachel - Genesis 29:7
10. Priscilla - Acts 18:2-3
11. Rhoda - Acts 12:13
12. Rebekah's - Genesis 24:63
13. As a reward for valour - Judges 1:12-13
14. Martha - Luke 10:40
15. Herodias' - Mark 6:17-28
16. The Queen of Sheba - 2 Chronicles 9:1
17. Jael - Judges 4:21
18. Rahab - Joshua 6:23
19. Wine and anything unclean - Judges 13:4
20. Deborah - Judges 4:4

SECTION 2: DISCOVERY!

ONE
1. Judas - John 18:2
2. Alphaeus - Matthew 10:3
3. Matthias - Acts 1:15-26
4. Elijah - Matthew 17:3
5. Simon - Matthew 10:2

Answer: James (Matthew 10:3)

TWO
1. Jonah - Jonah 1:3
2. Omega - Revelation 1:8
3. Abiathar - 1 Samuel 23:9
4. Simon - Matthew 10:4
5. Hannah - I Samuel 1:1-2

Answer: Joash (2 Chronicles 22:10-23)

THREE
1. Dorcas - Acts 9:36
2. Abba - Romans 8:15
3. Naboth - I Kings 21:1-14
4. Issachar - Genesis 30:18
5. Ephraim - Genesis 41:52
6. Lily - Luke 12:27

Answer: Daniel

FOUR
1. Apollos - Acts 18: 24-28
2. Naaman - 2 Kings 5
3. Timothy - Acts 16-20
4. Ish-Bosheth - 2 Samuel 2:10 - 4:12

5. Omri - 1 Kings 16:21-28
6. Cain - Genesis 4:1
7. Hosanna - Matthew 21:9, Mark 11:9, John 12:13
Answer: Antioch (Acts 11:20-21)

FIVE
1. Myrrh - Matthew 2:11
2. Isaiah - Isaiah 1:1
3. Zophar - Job 2:11
4. Pearl - Matthew 13:46
5. Abigail - 1 Samuel 25:14
6. Hiram - 2 Samuel 5:11
Answer: Mizpah (1 Samuel 7:5-6)

SIX
1. Gabriel - Daniel 8:16, 9:21
2. Ophir - 1 Kings 9:28
3. Leviticus
4. Ishmael - Genesis 16:15; Isaac 21:3.
5. Agabus - Acts 11:28
6. Thessalonians
7. Harp - Psalm 137:2
Answer: Goliath (1 Samuel 17:4)

SEVEN
1. Meshach - Daniel 3:21
2. Incense - Leviticus 2:1
3. Centurian - Acts 10:1
4. Hebron - Joshua 14:13, 15:13
5. Ahaz - 2 Kings 16
6. Laban - Genesis 29
Answer: Michal - (1 Samuel 14:49)

EIGHT
1. Bethel - Genesis 28:19
2. Arimathea - Matthew 27:57-60
3. Redeemer - Isaiah 49:26
4. Nazareth - Matthew 2:23
5. Aristarchus - Acts 19:29
6. Bartimaeus - Mark 10:46-52
7. Asher - Genesis 30:13
8. Sadducees - Acts 23:7,8

Answer: Barnabas (Acts 13:2)

NINE
1. Jesse - 1 Samuel 16:11
2. Ephesus - Acts 18:19-20; Revelation 2:1
3. Ruth
4. Isaiah - Isaiah 1:1
5. Cloud - Exodus 13:21
6 Herod - Matthew 2:16
7. Onesimus - Philemon

Answer: Jericho

TEN
1. Theophilus - Luke 1:3, Acts1:1
2. Ichabod - 1 Samuel 4:21
3. Thaddeus - Matthew 10:3
4. Ur - Genesis 11:28
5. Synagogue

Answer: Titus

ELEVEN
1. Virgins - Matthew 25:1
2. Asherah - Judges 3:7

3. Sycamore - Luke 19:4
4. Hebrews 11
5. Tiberias - John 6:23
6. Iscariot - Matthew 10:4

Answer: Vashti (Esther 1)

TWELVE
1. Purim - Esther 9:26
2. Revelation
3. Orpah - Ruth 1:14-15
4. Vinegar John 19:29-30
5. Eden - Genesis 2:8
6. Rainbow - Genesis 9:13-15
7. Bartholemew - Matthew 10:3
8. Sheba - 1 Kings 10

Answer: Proverbs

THIRTEEN
1. Zion
2. Adam
3. Didymus - John 20:24
4. Onyx - Exodus 28:20
5. Kedar - Genesis 25:13

Answer: Zadok (2 Samuel 8:17)

FOURTEEN
1. Salt - Matthew 5:13
2. Alpha
3. Mustard - Mark 4:30-32
4. Athaliah - 2 Kings 8:26
5. Rachel - Genesis 29:28
6. Israel - Genesis 32:28

7. Athens - Acts 17:15

Answer: Samaria

FIFTEEN
1. Manasseh - Genesis 41:51
2. Oak - Isaiah 2:13
3. Salome - Mark 16:1
4. Eunice - 2 Timothy 1:5
5. Serpent - Genesis 3:14

Answer: Moses

SIXTEEN
1. Philip - Matthew 10:3
2. Sarah - Genesis 17:15
3. Aquila - Acts 18:3
4. Leviathan - Job 3:8
5. Melchizedek - Hebrews 7:2
6. Samson - Judges 16:5

Answer: Psalms

SEVENTEEN
1. Ananias - Acts 9:10
2. Rhoda - Acts 12:13
3. Abednego - Daniel 1:7
4. Reuben - Genesis 29:32
5. Abner - 1 Samuel 14:50-51
6. Thyatira - Revelation 2:18

Answer: Ararat (Genesis 8:4)

EIGHTEEN
1. Absalom - 2 Samuel 3:3
2. Dead Sea
3. Uriah - 2 Samuel 23:39
4. Luke - Colossians 4:14

5. Luz - Genesis 28:19
6. Ahijah - 1 Kings 11:28-39
7. Methuselah - Genesis 5:27

Answer: Adullam - (Isaiah 22:1)

NINETEEN
1. Jordan
2. Obadiah - 1 Kings 18:4,13
3. Scorpion - Deuteronomy 8:15
4. Immanuel - Matthew 1:23
5. Arrow - 2 Kings 13:17
6. Habakkuk

Answer: Josiah (2 Kings 22)

TWENTY
1. Isaac - Genesis 21:5
2. Shekinah
3. Achan - Joshua 7
4. Issachar - Genesis 30:18
5. Adam - Genesis 2:20
6. Hagar - Genesis 16:1

Answer: Isaiah

TWENTY-ONE
1. Sermon on the Mount - Matthew 5-7
2. Ivory - 1 Kings 10:18-20
3. Lukewarm - Revelation 3:16
4. Ass - Numbers 22:30
5. Shekel

Answer: Silas (Acts 15:40)

TWENTY-TWO
1. Sword - Revelation 1:16
2. Artemis - Acts 19:23-41
3. Macedonia - Acts 16:9-10
4. Saul - 1 Samuel 10:24
5. Oil - Exodus 30:31
6. Naphtali - Genesis 30:8

Answer: Samson (Judges 16)

TWENTY-THREE
1. Deborah - Judges 4
2. Astrologers - Daniel 2:4
3. Vine - John 15:1
4. I am who I am - Exodus 3:14
5. Dagon - Judges 16:23

Answer: David (1 Samuel 16:13)

TWENTY-FOUR
1. Nabal - 1 Samuel 25:10
2. Onesiphorus - 2 Timothy 1:16
3. Annas - John 18:13,24
4. Hyssop - Exodus 12:22

Answer: Noah (Genesis 6:9)

TWENTY-FIVE
1. Jezebel - 1 Kings 16:31
2. Eloi - Mark 15:34
3. Talmud
4. Ham - Genesis 9:22
5. Rebekah - Genesis 24:67
6. Obadiah

Answer: Jethro (Exodus 3:1)

SECTION 3: HIDDEN NAMES

1 BIBLE CHARACTERS
1. Seth - Genesis 5:3
2. Tamar - 2 Samuel 13
3. Ham - Genesis 7:13
4. Levi - Mark 2:14
5. Abel - Genesis 4:2
6. Esau - Genesis 25:26
7. Andrew - Matthew 10:2
8. Amos - Amos 1:1
9. Dorcas - Acts 9:39
10. Anna - Luke 2:36

2 BOOKS OF THE BIBLE
1. Esther
2. James
3. Nahum
4. Kings
5. Hosea
6. Titus
7. Peter
8. Acts
9. Ruth
10. Job

3 BIBLE FOOD
1. Wheat - Amos 8:6
2. Melon - Numbers 11:5
3. Broth - Judges 6:20
4. Honey - Judges 14:8

5. Grapes - Numbers 13:23-24
6. Bread - Deuteronomy 8:3
7. Butter - Psalm 55:21
8. Raisins - 1 Samuel 30:12
9. Garlic - Numbers 11:5
10. Manna - Exodus 16

4 TREES IN THE BIBLE
1. Fir - Isaiah 60:13
2. Oak - 2 Samuel 18:10
3. Almond - Jeremiah 1:11
4. Pine - Isaiah 60:13
5. Cedar - 1 Kings 5:6

SECTION 4: FILL THE GAPS

1 FAMOUS A'S
1 Abba 2 Abednego 3 Abigail 4 Abraham 5 Achor
6 Adullam 7 Alpha 8 Ananias 9 Ararat 10 Athens

2 FAMOUS J's
1 Jezebel 2 Jude 3 Jairus 4 Jeremiah 5 Jerusalem
6 Jesse 7 Jethro 8 Jordan 9 Joshua 10 John the Baptist

3 FAMOUS P's
1 Paran 2 Patmos 3 Pentateuch 4 Philemon 5 Potiphar
6 Psalms 7 Philip 8 Philadelphia 9 Penuel 10 Philippi

4 FAMOUS R's
1 Rabbi 2 Rachel 3 Rainbow 4 Rebekah 5 Red Sea
6 Reuben 7 Rhoda 8 Ruth 9 Ramah 10 Redeemer

SECTION 5: LETTER AND NUMBER CODES

1   FOLLOWERS OF JESUS
1 Simon Peter 2 James 3 John 4 Matthew 5 Andrew 6 Philip 7 Bartholemew 8 Thomas 9 James Son of Alphaeus 10 Judas 11 Thaddeus 12 Martha 13 Mary 14 Lazarus 15 Joseph of Arimathea 16 Mary Magdalene 17 Joanna 18 Stephen 19 Matthias 20 Zacchaeus

2   NAMES OF GOD AND JESUS (1)
1 Bread of Life 2 Chief Cornerstone 3 First and Last 4 God of Glory 5 Great High Priest 6 Holy and True 7 King of Peace 8 Light of the World 9 Lord of All 10 Messiah 11 Morning Star 12 My Fortress 13 My Lamp 14 Our Potter 15 Precious Stone 16 Refiner and Purifier 17 Sanctuary 18 Shepherd 19 Sure Foundation 20 Vine

3   NAMES OF GOD AND JESUS (2)
1 Word of Life 2 Your Keeper 3 Strong Tower 4 Sun and Shield 5 Your Maker 6 Prince of Peace 7 Your Shield 8 Righteous Judge 9 Lion of Judah 10 Lord of Lords 11 Lord God of Truth 12 Image of God 13 Horn of Salvation 14 Flame 15 He Who Will Come 16 Eternal Life 17 Advocate 18 Deliverer 19 Crown of Glory 20 Father of Mercies

4   JEWISH FESTIVALS/FASTS
1 Purim 2 Tabernacles 3 Weeks 4 Unleavened Bread 5 The Sabbath 6 The Day of Blowing Trumpets 7 The Day of Atonement 8 Festival of Lights 9 Fast of Seventeenth of Tammuz 10 Fast of Tishah Be-ab

11 Fast of Gedeliah 12 Fast of Tenth of Tebet
13 Hoshanah Rabba 14 Shemini Rebet 15 Simhat
Torah

5 PAUL's JOURNEYS
1 Seleucia 2 Cyprus 3 Salamis 4 Paphos 5 Perga
6 Antioch 7 Iconium 8 Lystra 9 Derbe 10 Attalia
11 Cilicia 12 Syria 13 Philippi 14 Troas 15 Thessalonica
16 Ephesus 17 Athens 18 Berea 19 Corinth 20 Malta

6 PROPHETS AND PROPHETESSES
1 Abraham 2 Joel 3 Jonah 4 Isaiah 5 Micah 6 Jeremiah
7 Ezekiel 8 Malachi 9 Daniel 10 Nahum 11 Hosea
12 Amos 13 Haggai 14 Obadiah 15 Habakkuk
16 Zechariah 17 Elijah 18 Deborah 19 Elisha 20 Huldah

7 RIVERS, WATERWAYS, SEAS AND LAKES
1 Jordan 2 Galilee 3 Dead Sea 4 Nile 5 Euphrates
6 Red Sea 7 Tiberias 8 Tigris 9 Great Sea 10 Marah
11 Chinnereth 12 Abana 13 Menzaleth 14 Lake Timsah
15 Gihon 16 Pharphar 17 Kishon 18 Jabbok 19 Arnon
20 Kanah

8 VALLEYS IN THE BIBLE
1 Achor 2 Aijalon 3 Baca 4 Beracah 5 Elah 6 Siddim
7 Hinnom 8 Iphtah-El 9 Kings 10 Lebanon 11 Rephaim
12 Salt 13 Sorek 14 Jehoshaphat 15 Arnon 16 Shaveh
17 Esdraelon 18 Shephelah 19 Siloam 20 Tyropoeon

SECTION 6: ANAGRAMS

1   BIRDS IN THE BIBLE
1 Hawk 2 Swallow 3 Sparrow 4 Owl 5 Stork 6 Eagle
7 Vulture 8 Raven 9 Kite 10 Osprey 11 Cormorant
12 Gull 13 Heron 14 Quail 15 Partridge 16 Ostrich
17 Dove 18 Pigeon 19 Thrush 20 Swift

2   ANIMALS IN THE BIBLE
1 Mule 2 Camel 3 Goat 4 Lion 5 Leopard 6 Wolf
7 Hare 8 Weasel 9 Deer 10 Horse 11 Ass 12 Pigs
13 Donkey 14 Sheep 15 Bear 16 Fox 17 Mole
18 Mouse 19 Whale 20 Lizard

3   PLANTS, HERBS AND SPICES IN THE BI-
BLE

1 Mint 2 Dill 3 Cumin 4 Rue 5 Coriander 6 Mustard
7 Calamus 8 Cinnamon 9 Spikenard 10 Wormwood
11 Stacte 12 Onycha 13 Saffron 14 Hyssop 15 Man-
drake 16 Lily 17 Galbanum 18 Frankincense 19 Anise
20 Mallow

4   FOOD IN THE BIBLE
1 Pomegranate 2 Grapes 3 Cheese 4 Barley 5 Lentils
6 Cucumber 7 Apple 8 Millet 9 Onions 10 Melon
11 Beans 12 Garlic 13 Spelt 14 Butter 15 Almonds
16 Honey 17 Raisins 18 Fish 19 Leek 20 Fig

5   PRECIOUS AND SEMI-PRECIOUS STONES
1 Diamond 2 Emerald 3 Jasper 4 Sapphire 5 Pearl
6 Onyx 7 Chalcedony 8 Amethyst 9 Beryl 10 Ruby

11 Crystal 12 Agate 13 Carnelian 14 Yellow Quartz
15 Topaz 16 Turquoise 17 Garnet

6 KINGS IN THE BIBLE
1 Josiah 2 David 3 Ashab 4 Rehoboam 5 Solomon
6 Amaziah 7 Jehoash 8 Jehu 9 Ahaziah 10 Joash
11 Jeroboam 12 Jotham 13 Ahaz 14 Zechariah
15 Hezekiah 16 Manasseh 17 Jehoahaz 18 Jehoshaphat
19 Belshazzar 20 Artaxerxes

7 MOUNTAINS AND HILLS OF THE BIBLE
1 Ephraim 2 Olives 3 Ararat 4 Moriah 5 Zion 6 Nebo
7 Gilboa 8 Hermon 9 Horeb 10 Ebal 11 Carmel 12 Sinai
13 Gerizim 14 Paran 15 Gilead 16 Baalah 17 Moreh
18 Abarim 19 Hor 20 Tabor

SECTION 8: PAIRS

PAIRS 1
1   Abraham and Sarah
2   Aquila and Priscilla
3   Isaac and Rebekah
4   Moses and Zipporah
5   Boaz and Ruth
6   David and Bathsheba
7   Jacob and Leah
8   Adam and Eve
9   Amram and Jochebed
10   Zechariah and Elizabeth

PAIRS 2
1   Ananias and Sapphira

2 Ahab and Jezebel
3 Jacob and Rachel
4 Chuza and Joanna
5 Joseph and Asenath
6 Ahasuerus and Esther
7 Samson and Delilah
8 Aaron and Elisheba
9 Elkanah and Hannah
10 Elimelech and Naomi

PAIRS 3
1 James and John
2 Martha and Mary
3 Rachel and Leah
4 David and Jonathon
5 Esau and Jacob
6 Cain and Abel
7 Peter and Andrew
8 Philip and Herodias
9 Joshua and Caleb

PAIRS 4
1 Hagar and Ishmael
2 Hannah and Samuel
3 Elizabeth and John the Baptist
4 Eunice and Timothy
5 Sarah and Isaac
6 Ruth and Obed
7 Bathsheba and Solomon
8 Rachel and Joseph
9 Athaliah and King Ahaziah
10 Mary and Jesus

PAIRS 5

1 Cain and Enoch
2 Eli and Phinehas
3 Noah and Shem
4 Seth and Enosh
5 Saul and Jonathon
6 Nun and Joshua
7 Zebedee and James
8 Jeroboam and Abijah
9 Joash and Gideon
10 Solomon and Rehoboam

PAIRS 6

1 Hosea and Gomer
2 Johoida and Jehosheba
3 Lappidoth and Deborah
4 Silas and Paul
5 Jannes and Jambres
6 Felix and Drusilla
7 Agrippa and Bernice
8 Sodom and Gomorrah
9 Pharisee and the Tax Collector
10 Jonah and the Whale